Life Style Daily

한글 워크북

KOREAN WORKBOOK FOR BEGINNERS

© 2023 Life Style Daily. All rights reserved.

No part of this publication may be reproduced, distributed, or transmitted in any form or by any means, including photocopying, recording, or other electronic or mechanical methods, without the prior written permission of the publisher, except in the case of brief quotations embodied in critical reviews and certain other noncommercial uses permitted by copyright law. For permission requests, write to the publisher, addressed "Attention: Permissions Coordinator," at the address provided by Life Style Daily.

Unauthorized use and/or duplication of this material without express and written permission from Life Style Daily is strictly prohibited. Violators will be prosecuted to the fullest extent of the law.

1. Get to Know the Hangeul Alphabet

Start by familiarizing yourself with the basic elements of the Hangeul alphabet. It consists of 14 consonants and 10 vowels that can be combined to form syllables. Understanding the structure and sounds is crucial before you move on to writing practice.

2. Gather Your Tools

For Hangeul calligraphy, you need a few basic tools:

Calligraphy Brush - traditionally made from natural hair.

Ink - you can use ready-made calligraphy ink or Chinese ink.

Paper - preferably thick and absorbent, special for calligraphy.

Pad - under the paper to prevent bleeding.

3. Basics of Holding the Brush

Holding the brush correctly is key. Hold the brush vertically, securing it between your thumb and index finger, while the other fingers stabilize the grip. The brush should be held lightly but firmly.

4. Learning the Strokes

Hangeul calligraphy consists of various strokes: vertical, horizontal, curved, etc. Begin by practicing these strokes separately, focusing on fluidity and pressure. This is the foundation upon which you will build letters.

5. Assembling Letters

After mastering basic strokes, start combining them to form individual letters. Practice each letter separately, repeating multiple times to achieve fluidity and consistency.

6. Creating Syllables

Once you feel comfortable writing individual letters, begin combining them into syllables. Hangeul is unique in that letters are grouped into syllabic blocks to form complete words.

7. Practice and Patience

Calligraphy requires time and patience. Don't be discouraged by initial difficulties. Regular practice is key to mastering Hangeul calligraphy.

8. Seek Inspiration

Watch the work of other calligraphers, attend workshops, or watch video tutorials. Inspiration from others can significantly speed up your learning process.

9. Develop Your Own Style

Once you've mastered the basics, experiment with different styles and techniques to find your unique expression through Hangeul calligraphy.

10. Enjoy the Process

Remember that calligraphy is not just a skill, but also a form of relaxation and meditation. Enjoy every stroke and moment spent with the brush in hand.

Hangeul (한글)

ㄱ (g/k)	ㄴ (n)	ㄷ (d/t)	ㄹ (r/l)	ㅁ (m)
ㅂ (b/p)	ㅅ (s)	ㅇ (ng)	ㅈ (j)	ㅊ (ch)
ㅋ (k)	ㅌ (t)	ㅍ (p)	ㅎ (h)	ㄲ (kk)
ㄸ (tt)	ㅃ (pp)	ㅆ (ss)	ㅉ (jj)	ㅏ (a)
ㅑ (ya)	ㅓ (eo)	ㅕ (yeo)	ㅗ (o)	ㅛ (yo)
ㅜ (u)	ㅠ (yu)	ㅡ (eu)	ㅣ (i)	ㅐ (ae)
ㅒ (yae)	ㅔ (e)	ㅖ (ye)	ㅘ (wa)	ㅙ (wae)
ㅚ (oe)	ㅝ (wo)	ㅞ (we)	ㅟ (wi)	ㅢ (ui)

Lettering Exercise

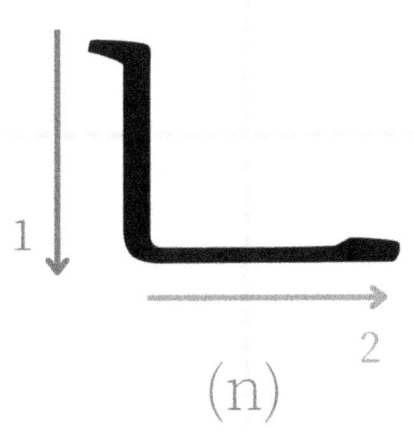

(n)

WORDS FROM "ㄴ"
- 나비 = butterfly
- 나무 = tree
- 네모 = square
- 눈 = eye

Lettering Exercise

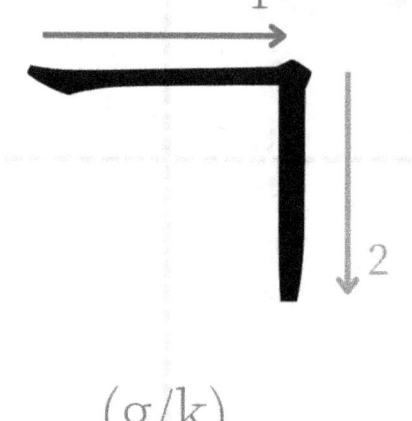

WORDS FROM "ㄱ"

- 가방 = bag
- 구두 = shoe
- 가위 = scissor
- 교실 = classroom

(g/k)

Lettering Exercise

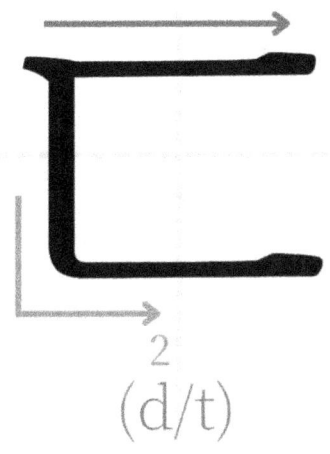

(d/t)

WORDS FROM "ㄷ"

- 독일 = Germany
- 동전 = coin
- 뒤로 = back
- 듣다 = listen

Lettering Exercise

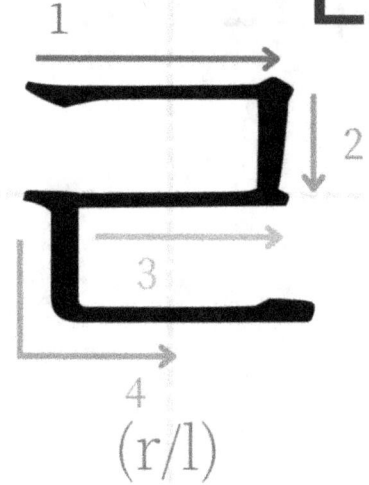

(r/l)

WORDS FROM "ㄹ"

- 러시아 = Russia
- 라디오 = radio
- 라면 = ramyeon
- 로봇 = robot

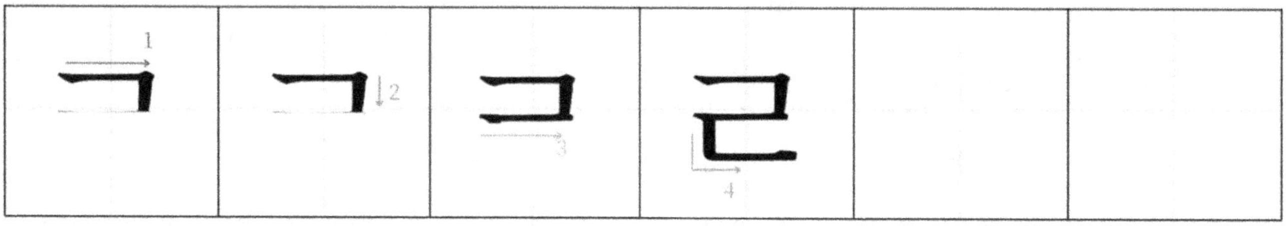

Lettering Exercise

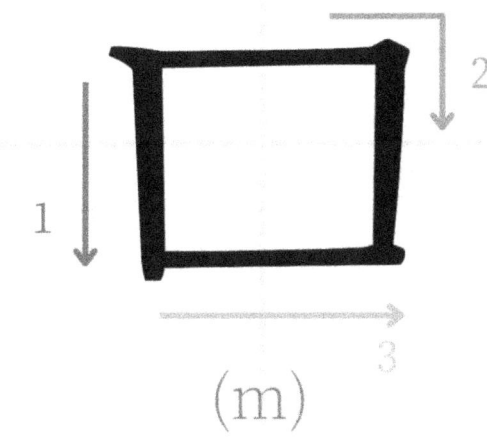

(m)

WORDS FROM "ㅁ"

- 물 = water
- 마시다 = drink
- 먹다 = eat
- 무엇 = what

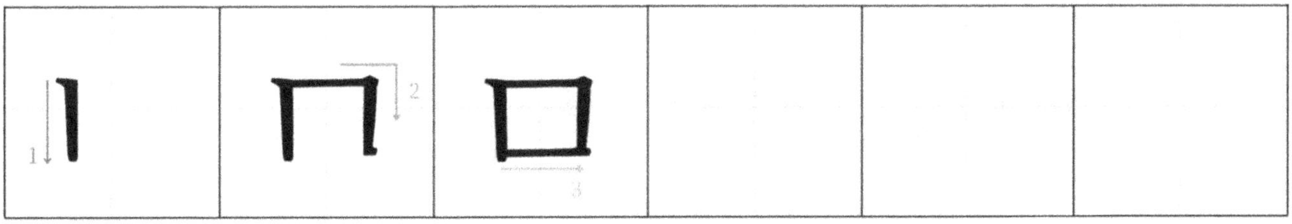

Lettering Exercise

WORDS FROM "ㅂ"

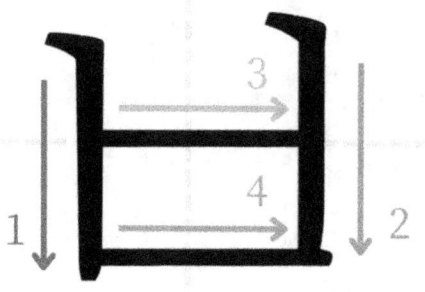

- 버스 = bus
- 바람 = wind
- 불 = fire
- 북쪽 = north

(b/p)

Lettering Exercise

WORDS FROM "ㅅ"

- 시간 = time
- 샤워 = shower
- 수영하다 = swim
- 슈팅 = shooting

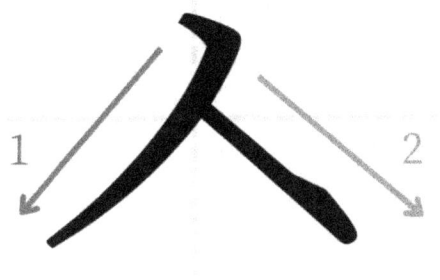

(s)

Lettering Exercise

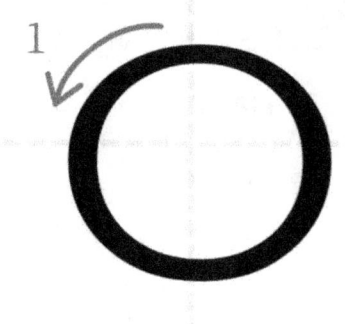

WORDS FROM "ㅇ"
- 얼마 = how much
- 어디 = where
- 어떤 = which
- 왜 = why

(ng)

Lettering Exercise

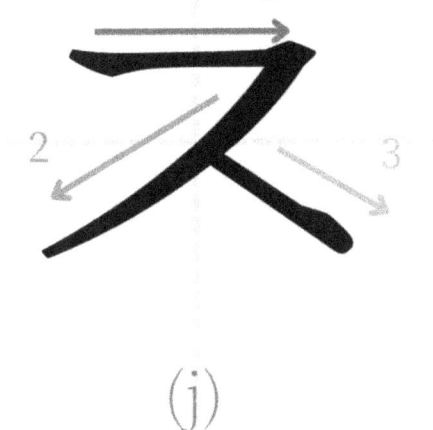

WORDS FROM "ㅈ"
- 자두 = plum
- 조개 = seashell
- 지도 = map
- 제비 = swallow

(j)

Lettering Exercise

WORDS FROM "ㅊ"

- 춤 = dance
- 침실 = bedroom
- 친구 = friend
- 치과 = dentist

(ch)

Lettering Exercise

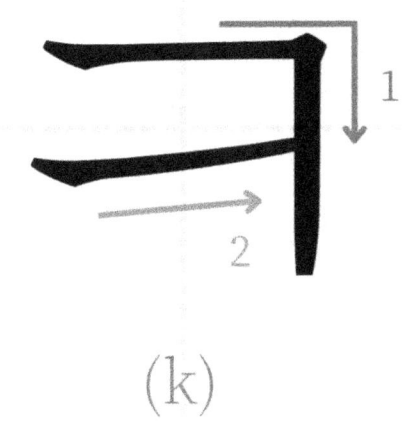

WORDS FROM "ㅋ"
- 커피 = coffee
- 코 = nose
- 케이크 = cake
- 카메라 = camera

(k)

Lettering Exercise

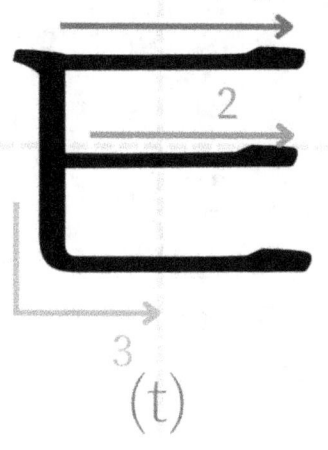

(t)

WORDS FROM "ㅌ"
- 태국 = Thailand
- 터키 = Turkey
- 타자기 = typewriter
- 타조 = ostrich

Lettering Exercise

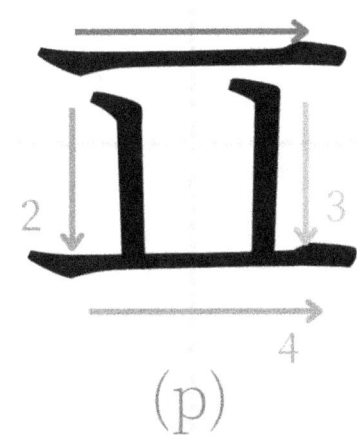

(p)

WORDS FROM "ㅍ"
- 파랑 = blue
- 팔 = arm
- 포도 = grape
- 파도 = waves

Lettering Exercise

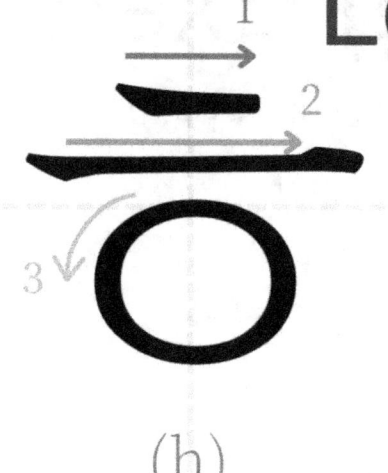

(h)

WORDS FROM "ㅎ"
- 학생 = student
- 행복 = happy
- 하다 = do
- 햇빛 = sunshine

Lettering Exercise

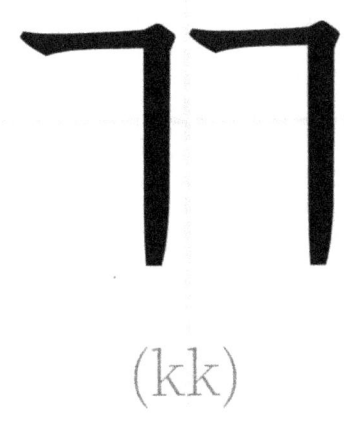

(kk)

WORDS FROM "ㄲ"
- 꽃 = flower
- 껌 = chewing gum
- 끝 = end
- 끊다 = hang up

ㄱ	ㄲ				

Lettering Exercise

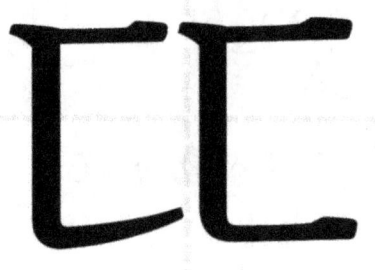

(tt)

WORDS FROM "ㄸ"
- 딸 = daughter
- 딸기 = strawberry
- 땅 = land
- 땅콩 = peanut

ㄷ	ㄸ				

Lettering Exercise

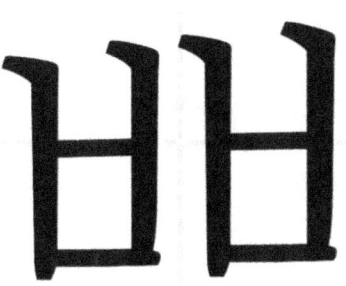

(pp)

WORDS FROM "ㅃ"
- 빵 = bread
- 뺨 = cheek
- 빨리 = fast
- 빨강 = red

ㅂ	ㅃ				

Lettering Exercise

WORDS FROM "ㅆ"

- 쓰다 = write
- 씨앗 = seed
- 쓰레기 = litter
- 싸다 = cheap

ㅆ

(ss)

Lettering Exercise

WORDS FROM "ㅉ"

- 찌개 = stew
- 짠 = salty
- 쪽지 = note
- 짝 = mate

(jj)

Lettering Exercise

WORDS FROM "ㅏ"

- 아저씨 = mister
- 안경 = glasses(specs)
- 앞 = front
- 아니요 = no

(a)

Lettering Exercise

ㅑ

(ya)

WORDS FROM "ㅑ"

- 양파= onion
- 양말= shocks
- 야채= vegetables
- 약간= a little

Lettering Exercise

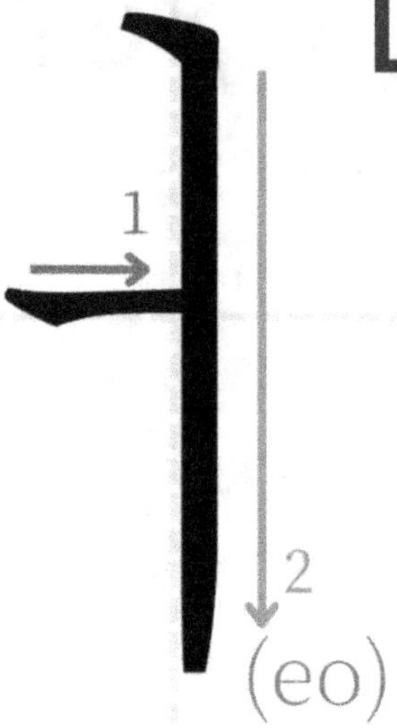

WORDS FROM "ㅓ"

- 언어 = language
- 엄마 = mom
- 억양 = accent
- 어금니 = molar

Lettering Exercise

ㅕ
(yeo)

WORDS FROM "ㅕ"
- 연필= pencil
- 영어= english
- 역사= history
- 여름= summer

Lettering Exercise

WORDS FROM "ㅗ"

- 오다 = come
- 오토바이 = motorbike
- 오늘 = today
- 오른쪽 = right

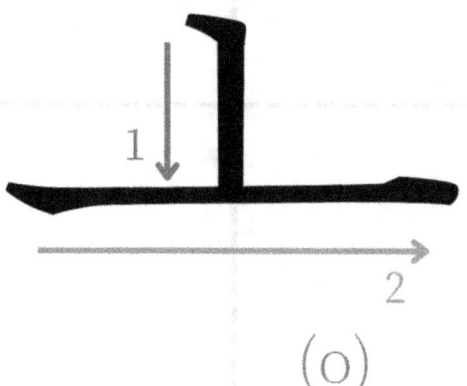

(o)

Lettering Exercise

ㅛ

WORDS FROM "ㅛ"

- 요리 = cook
- 요즘 = nowadays
- 용서 = forgiveness
- 용무 = business

(yo)

Lettering Exercise

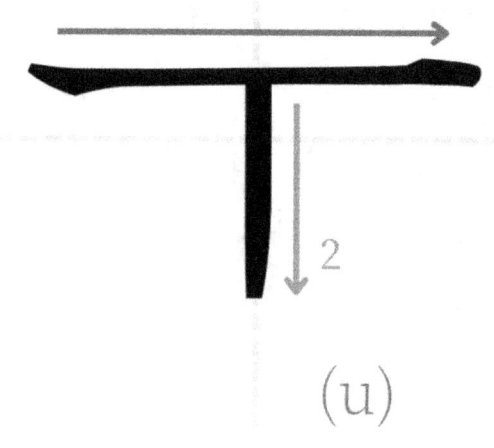

(u)

WORDS FROM "ㅜ"

- 우산 = umbrella
- 울다 = cry
- 웃다 = laugh
- 우유 = milk

Lettering Exercise

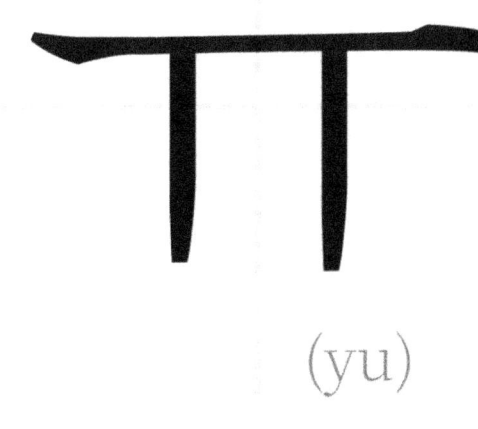

(yu)

WORDS FROM "ㅠ"
- 유도 = judo
- 휴가 = holiday
- 유튜브 = Youtube
- 공유하다 = share

Lettering Exercise

WORDS FROM "ㅡ"

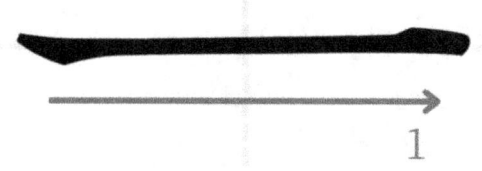

- 음악 = music
- 음식 = food
- 은행 = bank
- 음악회 = concert

(eu)

Lettering Exercise

ㅣ

WORDS FROM " ㅣ "

- 일 = day
- 일하다 = work
- 이름 = name
- 읽다 = read

1↓

(i)

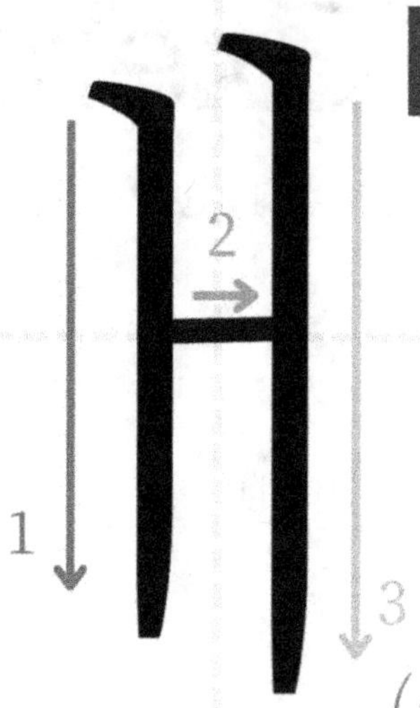

Lettering Exercise

WORDS FROM "ㅐ"

- 재미 = fun
- 개미 = ant
- 태양 = sun
- 천재 = genius

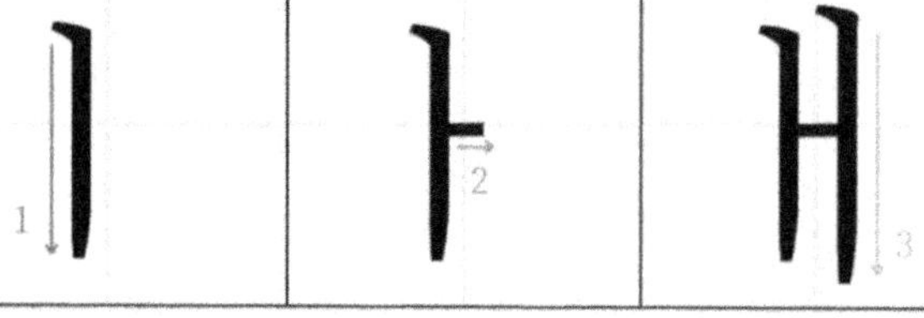

ㅐ (ae)

ㅒ Lettering Exercise

WORDS FROM "ㅒ"

- 얘기 = story
- 얘기꾼 = storyteller
- 얘들아 = guys
- 얘깃거리 = topic

(yae)

Lettering Exercise

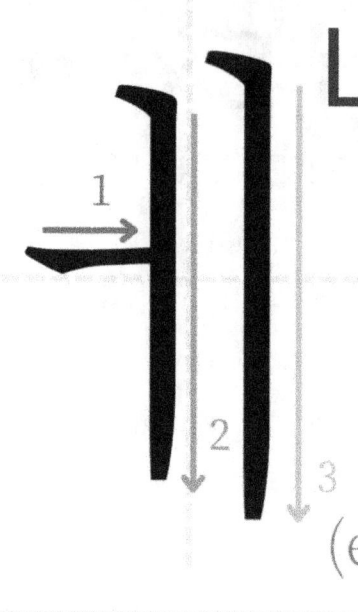

WORDS FROM "ㅔ"

- 에스프레소 = espresso
- 세수 = wash up
- 메뚜기 = grasshopper
- 세제 = detergent

ㅖ Lettering Exercise

WORDS FROM "ㅖ"
- 예쁜 = pretty
- 예약 = reservation
- 계단 = stairs
- 예시 = example

(ye)

ㅘ

(wa)

Lettering Exercise

WORDS FROM "ㅘ"

- 와인 = wine
- 관심 = interest
- 사과 = apple
- 화장실 = toilet

ㅗ	ㅘ				

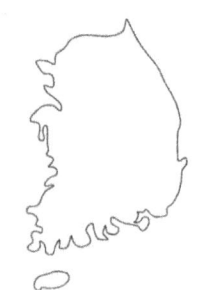

Lettering Exercise

왜

(wae)

WORDS FROM "왜"

- 돼지 = pig
- 쇄골 = collarbone
- 왜가리 = common hero

ㅗ	왜				

Lettering Exercise

ㅚ

(oe)

WORDS FROM "ㅚ"
- 회사 = company
- 열쇠 = key
- 왼쪽 = left
- 외국인 = foreigner

ㅗ	ㅚ				

Lettering Exercise

ㅝ
(wo)

WORDS FROM "ㅝ"
- 원숭이 = monkey
- 원피스 = dress
- 동물원 = zoo
- 파워 = power

ㅜ	ㅝ				

Lettering Exercise

ㅞ
(we)

WORDS FROM "ㅞ"
- 스웨터 = sweater
- 궤도 = orbit
- 웨딩 = wedding
- 췌장 = pancreas

ㅜ	ㅞ				

Lettering Exercise

WORDS FROM "ㅟ"

- 바위 = rock
- 키위 = kiwi
- 귀신 = ghost
- 바퀴 = wheel

wi)

ㅜ	ㅟ				

Lettering Exercise

ㅓ

(ui)

WORDS FROM "ㅢ"
- 의자 = chair
- 의사 = doctor
- 우의 = raincoat
- 의무 = duty

Numbers (숫자)

NATIVE KOREAN NUMBERS

1	하나 (hana)	9	아홉 (ahop)
2	둘 (dul)	10	열 (yeol)
3	셋 (set)		
4	넷 (net)		
5	다섯 (daseot)		
6	여섯 (yeoseot)		
7	일곱 (ilgop)		
8	여덟 (yeodeol)		

1하나 (hana)

하	나						
		1하나					

2둘 (dul)

둘							
			둘				

3 셋 (set)

셋							

4넷 (net)

넷							
			4넷				

5다섯 (daseot)

다	섯						

6 여섯 (yeoseot)

| 여 | 섯 | | | | | |

7 일곱 (ilgop)

일	곱						

8 여덟 (yeodeol)

여	덟						

9아홉 (ahop)

여	홉					

(empty practice grid)

| | | | | 아 | 홉 | |

10 열 (yeol)

열							

Numbers (숫자)

SINO-KOREAN NUMBERS

1	일 (il)	9	구 (gu)
2	이 (i)	10	십 (sip)
3	삼 (sam)		
4	사 (sa)		
5	오 (o)		
6	육 (yuk)		
7	칠 (chil)		
8	팔 (pal)		

1일 (il)

일							
				일			

2이 (i)

이

3삼 (sam)

삼							
			3삼				

4 사 (sa)

사							

5 오 (o)

오							
			오				

6 육 (yuk)

육							

7칠 (chil)

칠							

			칠				

8 팔 (pal)

팔							

9 구 (gu)

구							

10십 (sip)

십							
				십			

Exercise Pages | 연습 페이지

Exercise Pages | 연습 페이지

	ㅏ ㅏ ㅏ ㅏ ㅏ ㅏ
Name (a)	알았어	아니요
Read a	I Know	No
Pronunciation Father	ar-ass-eo	a-ni-yo

가
나
다
라
마
바
사
아
자
차
카
타
파
하

Exercise Pages | 연습 페이지

	ㅓ					
Name	(eo)	천만에요		저기요		
Read	eo	You're welcome		Excuse me		
Pronunciation	oh	cheon-man-e-yo		jeo-gi-yo		

거							
너							
더							
러							
머							
버							
서							
어							
저							
처							
커							
터							
퍼							
허							

Exercise Pages | 연습 페이지

Name: (ㅗ)
Read: o
Pronunciation: on

안 좋아요 — Not Good — an joh-a-yo

몰라요 — I don't know — mol-la-yo

고	고	고	고				
노	노	노	노				
도	도	도	도				
로	로	로	로				
모	모	모	모				
보	보	보	보				
소	소	소	소				
오	오	오	오				
조	조	조	조				
초	초	초	초				
코	코	코	코				
토	토	토	토				
포	포	포	포				
호	호	호	호				

Exercise Pages | 연습 페이지

Name	ㅜ (u)
Read	u
Pronunciation	Fl<u>u</u>

싱글룸 — A Single Room — sing-geul-l<u>u</u>m

체크아웃 — Check-out — che-keu-a-u<u>t</u>

구 누 두 루 무 부 수 우 주 추 쿠 투 푸 후

Exercise Pages | 연습 페이지

ー→1							
Name	**(eu)**	제 이름은		버 스			
Read	eu	My name is		Bus			
Pronunciation	Trag**e**dy	je i-reum-**eu**n		beo-s**eu**			

그	그	그	그				
느	ㄴ	ㄴ	ㄴ				
드	ㄷ	ㄷ	ㄷ				
르	ㄹ	ㄹ	ㄹ				
므	ㅁ	ㅁ	ㅁ				
브	ㅂ	ㅂ	ㅂ				
스	ㅅ	ㅅ	ㅅ				
으	ㅇ	ㅇ	ㅇ				
즈	ㅈ	ㅈ	ㅈ				
츠	ㅊ	ㅊ	ㅊ				
크	ㅋ	ㅋ	ㅋ				
트	ㅌ	ㅌ	ㅌ				
프	ㅍ	ㅍ	ㅍ				
흐	ㅎ	ㅎ	ㅎ				

Exercise Pages | 연습 페이지

Name	(i)	이해해요	비상
Read	i	I Understand	Emergency
Pronunciation	M<u>i</u>nute	<u>i</u>-hae-hae-yo	b<u>i</u>-sang

기			
니			
디			
리			
미			
비			
시			
이			
지			
치			
키			
티			
피			
히			

Exercise Pages | 연습 페이지

ㅐ	ㅐ ㅐ ㅐ ㅐ ㅐ ㅐ

Name	(ae)	맥 주	아 내
Read	ae	Beer	Wife
Pronunciation	D<u>ay</u>	m<u>ae</u>k-ju	a-n<u>ae</u>

개	개	개	개				
내	내	내	내				
대	대	대	대				
래	래	래	래				
매	매	매	매				
배	배	배	배				
새	새	새	새				
애	애	애	애				
재	재	재	재				
채	채	채	채				
캐	캐	캐	캐				
태	태	태	태				
패	패	패	패				
해	해	해	해				

Exercise Pages | 연습 페이지

Name	ㅔ (e)	네	어제
Read	e	Yes	Yesterday
Pronunciation	End	ne	eo-je

게
네
데
레
메
베
세
에
제
체
케
태
패
해

Complex Vowels

Exercise Pages | 연습 페이지

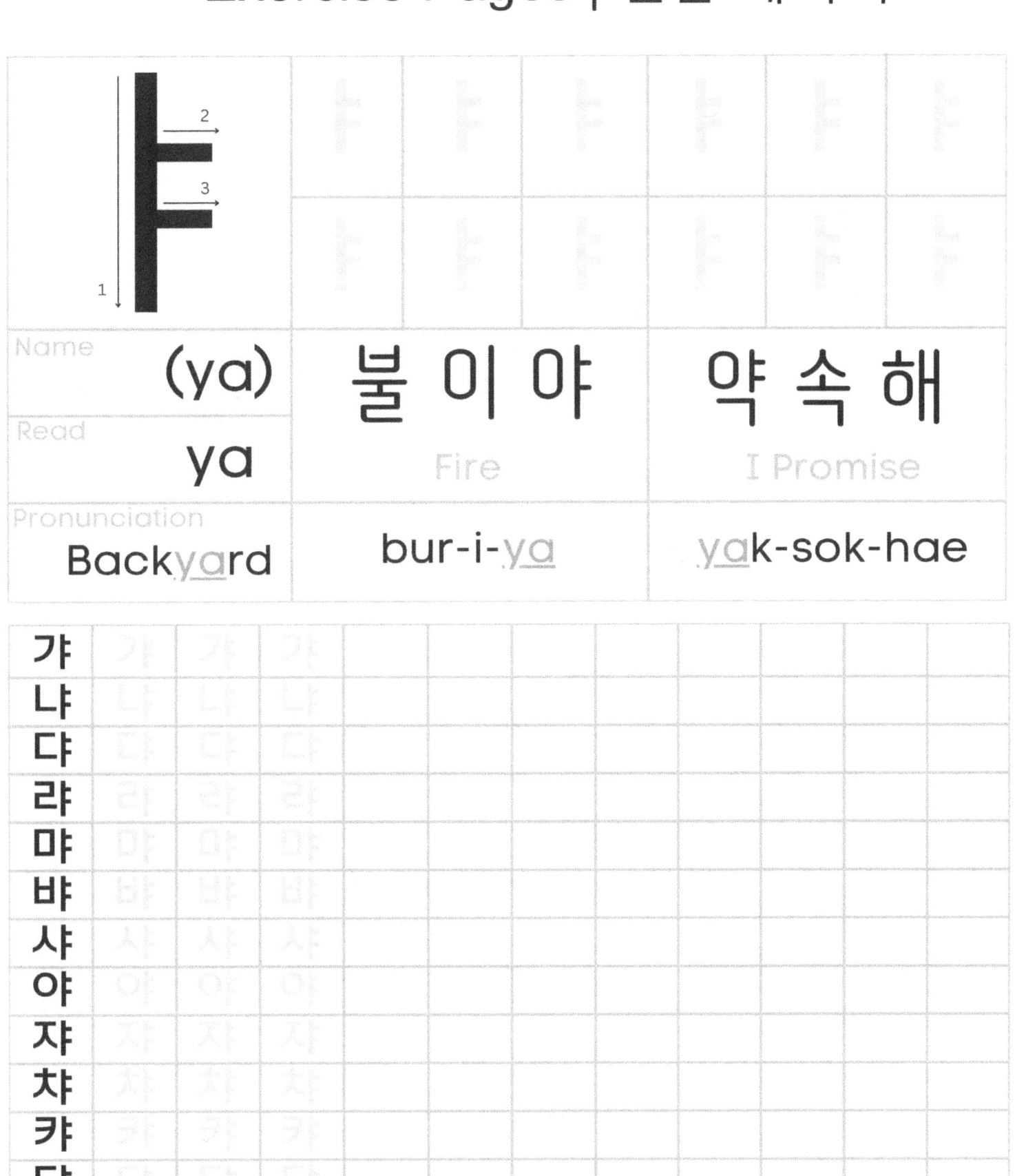

Exercise Pages | 연습 페이지

Name: (yeo)
Read: yeo
Pronunciation: y<u>u</u>p

ㅕ ㅕ ㅕ ㅕ ㅕ ㅕ
ㅕ ㅕ ㅕ ㅕ ㅕ ㅕ

경찰	여자친구
Police	Girlfriend
g<u>yeo</u>ng-chal	<u>yeo</u>-ja-chin-gu

겨	겨	겨	겨			
녀	녀	녀	녀			
뎌	뎌	뎌	뎌			
려	려	려	려			
며	며	며	며			
벼	벼	벼	벼			
셔	셔	셔	셔			
여	여	여	여			
져	져	져	져			
쳐	쳐	쳐	쳐			
켜	켜	켜	켜			
텨	텨	텨	텨			
펴	펴	펴	펴			
혀	혀	혀	혀			

Exercise Pages | 연습 페이지

ㅛ	ㅛ	ㅛ	ㅛ	ㅛ	ㅛ	ㅛ
	ㅛ	ㅛ	ㅛ	ㅛ	ㅛ	ㅛ

Name	(yo)	주세요	쇼핑
Read	yo	Please	Shopping
Pronunciation	Yogurt	ju-se-yo	syo-ping

교	교	교	교			
뇨	뇨	뇨	뇨			
됴	됴	됴	됴			
료	료	료	료			
묘	묘	묘	묘			
뵤	뵤	뵤	뵤			
쇼	쇼	쇼	쇼			
요	요	요	요			
죠	죠	죠	죠			
쵸	쵸	쵸	쵸			
쿄	쿄	쿄	쿄			
툐	툐	툐	툐			
표	표	표	표			
효	효	효	효			

Exercise Pages | 연습 페이지

ㅠ	ㅠ	ㅠ	ㅠ	ㅠ	ㅠ	ㅠ
	ㅠ	ㅠ	ㅠ	ㅠ	ㅠ	ㅠ

Name	(yu)	유 방	근 육
Read	yu	Breast	Muscles
Pronunciation	<u>You</u>th	.yu-bang	khun-.yun

규							
뉴							
듀							
류							
뮤							
뷰							
슈							
유							
쥬							
츄							
큐							
튜							
퓨							
휴							

Exercise Pages | 연습 페이지

ㅐ		
Name (yae)	애들아	얘기해
Read yae	Guys	Talk To Me
Pronunciation Yay!	yae-deul-a	yae-gi-hae

개
내
댸
래
먜
뱨
섀
얘
쟤
챼
컈
턔
퍠
해

Exercise Pages | 연습 페이지

ㅖ		
Name (ye)	시 계	예
Read ye	Watch	Yes
Pronunciation Yay!	si-gye	ye

계
녜
뎨
례
몌
볘
셰
예
졔
쳬
켸
톄
폐
혜

Exercise Pages | 연습 페이지

와 (wa)

Name: (wa)
Read: wa
Pronunciation: G**ua**va

와 요	와 함께
Come	With
wa-yo	**wa**-ham-kke

과
놔
돠
롸
뫄
봐
솨
와
좌
촤
콰
톼
퐈
화

Exercise Pages | 연습 페이지

외

Name: (oe)
Read: oe
Pronunciation: Wearable

외국인	외국
Foreigner	Foreign Country
oegug-in	oe-gug

- 괴
- 뇌
- 되
- 뢰
- 뫼
- 뵈
- 소
- 외
- 죄
- 최
- 쾨
- 퇴
- 푀
- 회

Exercise Pages | 연습 페이지

왜

Name: (wae)
Read: wae
Pronunciation: Wear

왜 그래	왜요?
Whats Wrong?	Why?
wae geu-lae	wae-yo?

괘
놰
돼
뢔
뫠
봬
쇄
왜
좨
쵀
쾌
퇘
퐤
화

Exercise Pages | 연습 페이지

워		
Name: (wo)	워 크	뭐 야
Read: wo	Work	What
Pronunciation: <u>Wo</u>n't	<u>wo</u>-keu	m<u>wo</u>-ya

궈
눠
둬
뤄
뭐
붜
숴
워
줘
춰
쿼
퉈
풔
휘

Exercise Pages | 연습 페이지

위	위	위	위	위	위	위
	위	위	위	위	위	위

Name	(wi)	위 치	위 해
Read	wi	Location	For
Pronunciation	Wings	wi-chi	wi-hae

귀			
뉘			
뒤			
뤼			
뮈			
뷔			
쉬			
위			
쥐			
취			
퀴			
튀			
퓌			
휘			

Exercise Pages | 연습 페이지

웨

Name	(we)
Read	we
Pronunciation	Weather

웨이터 — Waitor — we-i-teo

스웨터 — Sweater — seu-we-teo

괘			
눼			
뒈			
뤠			
뭬			
붸			
쉐			
웨			
줴			
췌			
퀘			
퉤			
풰			
훼			

Exercise Pages | 연습 페이지

의

Name	(ui)
Read	ui
Pronunciation	William

의사 — Doctor — ui-sa

의자 — Chair — ui-ja

귀
뉘
뒤
뤼
뮈
뷔
쉬
위
쥐
취
퀴
튀
퓌
휘

Single Consonants

Exercise Pages | 연습 페이지

Exercise Pages | 연습 페이지

ㄴ	ㄴ ㄴ ㄴ ㄴ ㄴ
Name (니은, nieun)	친구 / Friend — chin-gu	예쁘네요 / You are pretty — ye-ppeu-ne-yo
Read n		
Pronunciation <u>N</u>one		

나	나	나	나
너	너	너	너
노	노	노	노
누	누	누	누
느	느	느	느
니	니	니	니
내	내	내	내
네	네	네	네
냐	냐	냐	냐
녀	녀	녀	녀
뇨	뇨	뇨	뇨
뉴	뉴	뉴	뉴
내	내	내	내
녜	녜	녜	녜

Exercise Pages | 연습 페이지

다							
더							
도							
두							
드							
디							
대							
데							
댜							
뎌							
됴							
듀							
댸							
뎨							

Exercise Pages | 연습 페이지

ㄹ						
Name (리을, rieul)	물 Water		사 람 Human			
Read l/r						
Pronunciation **L**amp	mu**l**		sa-**r**-am			

라							
러							
로							
루							
르							
리							
래							
레							
랴							
려							
료							
류							
럐							
례							

Exercise Pages | 연습 페이지

Name (미음, mieum)	정 말 — Really	가 끔 — Sometimes
Read m		
Pronunciation Mold	jeong-mal	ga-kkeum

| 마 |
| 머 |
| 모 |
| 무 |
| 므 |
| 미 |
| 매 |
| 메 |
| 야 |
| 며 |
| 묘 |
| 뮤 |
| 먜 |
| 몌 |

Exercise Pages | 연습 페이지

ㅂ	Name (비읍, bieup)	비상	아빠
	Read **p/b**	Emergency	Dad
	Pronunciation **P**erson	**b**i-sang	a-**pp**a

바			
버			
보			
부			
브			
비			
배			
베			
뱌			
벼			
뵤			
뷰			
뱨			
볘			

Exercise Pages | 연습 페이지

ㅅ						
Name (시옷, sieut)	사 랑		어 디 서			
Read s	Love		Where			
Pronunciation Same	sa-rang		eo-di-so			

사								
서								
소								
수								
스								
시								
새								
세								
샤								
셔								
쇼								
슈								
섀								
셰								

Exercise Pages | 연습 페이지

ㅇ (1, 2)	ㅇ ㅇ ㅇ ㅇ ㅇ ㅇ
Name (이응, ieung) **Read** silent/ng **Pronunciation** Maki**ng**	빵 — Bread — ppa**ng** 아빠 — Dad — _a-ppa

아	아	아	아
어	어	어	어
오	오	오	오
우	우	우	우
으	으	으	으
이	이	이	이
애	애	애	애
에	에	에	에
야	야	야	야
여	여	여	여
요	요	요	요
유	유	유	유
얘	얘	얘	얘
예	예	예	예

Exercise Pages | 연습 페이지

ㅈ (지읒, jieut)

Read: j

Pronunciation: **J**ack

저기요 — Excuse Me — jeo-gi-yo

소주 — Soju — so-ju

자 저 조 주 즈 지 재 제 쟈 져 죠 쥬 쟤 졔

Exercise Pages | 연습 페이지

ㅊ		
Name (치읓, chieut)	야채	친구
Read ch	Vegetables	Friend
Pronunciation Chain	ya-chae	chin-gu

차			
처			
초			
추			
츠			
치			
채			
체			
챠			
쳐			
쵸			
츄			
챼			
쳬			

Exercise Pages | 연습 페이지

ㅋ						
Name (키읔, kieuk)	커피		결코			
Read: k	Coffee		Never			
Pronunciation: **K**ey	**k**eo-pi		gyeol-**k**o			

카							
커							
코							
쿠							
크							
키							
캐							
케							
캬							
켜							
쿄							
큐							
컈							
켸							

Exercise Pages | 연습 페이지

ㅌ (1,2,3,4 strokes)	ㅌ	ㅌ	ㅌ	ㅌ	ㅌ
	ㅌ	ㅌ	ㅌ	ㅌ	ㅌ

Name	(티읕, tieut)	택시	손톱
Read	t	Taxi	Fingernail
Pronunciation	**T**ake	**t**aeg-si	son-**t**ob

타	타	타	타
터	터	터	터
토	토	토	토
투	투	투	투
트	트	트	트
티	티	티	티
태	태	태	태
테	테	테	테
탸	탸	탸	탸
텨	텨	텨	텨
툐	툐	툐	툐
튜	튜	튜	튜
턔	턔	턔	턔
톄	톄	톄	톄

Exercise Pages | 연습 페이지

ㅍ (strokes 1, 2, 3, 4)	ㅍ	ㅍ	ㅍ	ㅍ	ㅍ	ㅍ
	ㅍ	ㅍ	ㅍ	ㅍ	ㅍ	ㅍ

Name (피읖, pieup)	피부	휴대폰
Read: **p**	Skin	Mobile Phone
Pronunciation: **P**andora	pi-bu	hyu-dae-pon

파	파	파	파					
퍼	퍼	퍼	퍼					
포	포	포	포					
푸	푸	푸	푸					
프	프	프	프					
피	피	피	피					
패	패	패	패					
페	페	페	페					
퍄	퍄	퍄	퍄					
펴	펴	펴	펴					
표	표	표	표					
퓨	퓨	퓨	퓨					
퍠	퍠	퍠	퍠					
폐	폐	폐	폐					

Exercise Pages | 연습 페이지

ㅎ (stroke order 1,2,3,4)	화장실	천천히
Name (히읗, hieuh)	Bathroom	Slowly
Read h		
Pronunciation **H**orror	**h**wa-jang-sil	cheon-cheon-**h**i

하	하	하	하
허	허	허	허
호	호	호	호
후	후	후	후
흐	흐	흐	흐
히	히	히	히
해	해	해	해
헤	헤	헤	헤
햐	햐	햐	햐
혀	혀	혀	혀
효	효	효	효
휴	휴	휴	휴
햬	햬	햬	햬
혜	혜	혜	혜

Double Consonants

Exercise Pages | 연습 페이지

ㄲ	ㄲ	ㄲ	ㄲ	ㄲ	ㄲ	ㄲ
	ㄲ	ㄲ	ㄲ	ㄲ	ㄲ	ㄲ

Name (쌍기역, ssanggiyeok)	떡볶이	꿀
Read: kk	Rice Cakes	Honey
Pronunciation: Ski	tteok-bokk-i	kkul

까	까	까	까				
꺼	꺼	꺼	꺼				
꼬	꼬	꼬	꼬				
꾸	꾸	꾸	꾸				
끄	끄	끄	끄				
끼	끼	끼	끼				
깨	깨	깨	깨				
께	께	께	께				
꺄	꺄	꺄	꺄				
껴	껴	껴	껴				
꾜	꾜	꾜	꾜				
뀨	뀨	뀨	뀨				
깨	깨	깨	깨				
꼐	꼐	꼐	꼐				

Exercise Pages | 연습 페이지

ㄸ						
Name (쌍디귿, ssangdigeut)	딸		땅콩			
Read: tt	Daughter		Peanut			
Pronunciation: Ki**tt**en	**dd**al		**tt**ang-kong			

따						
떠						
또						
뚜						
뜨						
띠						
때						
떼						
땨						
뗘						
뚀						
뜌						
떄						
떼						

Exercise Pages | 연습 페이지

ㅃ						
Name (쌍비읍, ssangbieup)	아 빠		뽀 뽀			
Read: pp	Dad		Kiss			
Pronunciation: Apartment	appa		ppoppo			

빠											
뻐											
뽀											
뿌											
쁘											
삐											
빼											
뻬											
뺘											
뼈											
뾰											
쀼											
뺴											
뼤											

Exercise Pages | 연습 페이지

ㅉ						
Name (쌍지읒, ssangjieut)	짜장면 Black Bean Noodles		진짜 Really			
Read: jj	jja-jang-myeon		jin-jja			
Pronunciation: Jim						

짜											
쩌											
쪼											
쭈											
쯔											
찌											
째											
쩨											
쨔											
쪄											
쪼											
쮸											
쨰											
쪠											

Exercise Pages | 연습 페이지

ㅆ	ㅆ	ㅆ	ㅆ	ㅆ	ㅆ	ㅆ
	ㅆ	ㅆ	ㅆ	ㅆ	ㅆ	ㅆ

Name (쌍시옷, ssangsiot)	쑥	싸우다
Read: ss	Mugwort	Fight
Pronunciation: Su**sh**i	**ss**uk	**ss**a-u-da

싸	싸	싸	싸							
써	써	써	써							
쏘	쏘	쏘	쏘							
쓰	쓰	쓰	쓰							
쓰	쓰	쓰	쓰							
씨	씨	씨	씨							
쌔	쌔	쌔	쌔							
쎄	쎄	쎄	쎄							
쌰	쌰	쌰	쌰							
쎠	쎠	쎠	쎠							
쑈	쑈	쑈	쑈							
쓔	쓔	쓔	쓔							
썌	썌	썌	썌							
쎼	쎼	쎼	쎼							

Exercise Pages | 연습 페이지

Exercise Pages | 연습 페이지

Exercise Pages | 연습 페이지

Exercise Pages | 연습 페이지

Korean Workbook for Beginners: A Guide to Getting Started

We appreciate the time and effort you've invested in exploring the "Korean Workbook for Beginners." Your commitment to mastering the art of Korean calligraphy has been an inspiration to us all. As you continue on this artistic path, we're excited to see where your talents will take you.

Warm wishes,

The "Life Style Daily" Team

www.ingramcontent.com/pod-product-compliance
Lightning Source LLC
LaVergne TN
LVHW060334080526
838202LV00053B/4473